Acknowledgements

I am so grateful to the many people that made my dream become a reality. Lori Alexander worked closely with me in writing this children's book. My college friend, Carol Keeney, inspired me after the writing of her first book, *Brand New Teacher*, while her husband Joe Keeney, gave me countless hours of his time formatting this book and walking me through the process of self publishing. In addition I thank my husband, Ted, my children, and many friends, who have given suggestions along the way.

A great big thank you goes to Vladimir Cebu, my illustrator, for his extraordinary work. I trust his illustrations will bless many.

My desire is that through Gabe's message we will seek opportunities for God to use us all.

Dedication

This book is dedicated in memory of Cristen Alexander, who brought special messages to many people, possibly just like Gabe did.

God's Special Messenger

By Roberta Meier
In collaboration with Loretta Alexander
Illustrations by Vladimir Cebu

CONFRERE PUBLISHING
Cornelius, North Carolina

God's Special Messenger

Confrere Publishing

16711 Jetton Road
Cornelius, North Carolina 28031

Email us at:
messengergabe2015@gmail.com

ISBN: 978-0-9968901-0-6

Notice of Rights

Disclaimer

Hi! I'm Gabriel. My friends call me Gabe. I am an angel.

You may have heard of me in God's book, the Bible.

God uses angels in many ways.

Let me tell you how He used me...

I was floating through heaven one day when I heard a voice.

The voice was God's.

"Gabriel," He said, "I have picked you to do a very special job for me."

I like when God speaks to me! I was thrilled when I heard that God wanted me to do a special job for HIM!

I listened carefully. "Gabriel," God explained, "I need you to go to a young girl. Her name is Mary."

"Tell her that I have chosen her to be the mother of my son. She will give birth to Him and is to name the baby, Jesus."

What a message God wanted me to give to Mary! Would Mary believe what I was telling her?

I knew what God wanted me to do, so I was off to find Mary to give her God's message.

When I found her she was alone. I whispered, "Psst… Mary, over here."

"Don't be afraid, Mary, I am Gabriel, one of God's angels. He has sent me to you with a special message."

"God has chosen you to be the mother of His Son. God wants you to name Him, JESUS."

"You and Joseph are to marry as planned. After some time you will give birth to JESUS."

Mary listened carefully to the message.

She wondered how this could happen, but Mary knew, with God, all things were possible!

God wanted Joseph to know His plan, so He sent me to him. When I arrived Joseph was sleeping.

I decided not to wake him. So I spoke to him in a dream.

"Joseph," I said softly, "God has sent me to you with a special message. He wants you to marry Mary. She is going to have a baby. This baby is God's Son. He wants you and Mary to name him, JESUS."

When Joseph awoke he remembered this dream. He did what God asked and married Mary.

Months passed and it was almost time for JESUS to be born.

One day Joseph was told that the king of the land wanted to count all men. The men were to go to the town where they had been born.

Joseph was born in a town named Bethlehem. He had to obey the king and go there. Joseph took Mary with him.

When Mary and Joseph arrived in Bethlehem, Joseph tried to find a place for them to sleep. All the rooms were filled, but there was a space for them to spend the night with the animals.

It was on this night, that God's Son, JESUS, was born. Mary wrapped Him in cloths and laid Him in a manger.

There were shepherds in the fields. An angel appeared to them, "God's Son has been born tonight in Bethlehem. You will find Him lying in a manger."

More angels appeared to the shepherds.
They praised God for sending His Son.

After the angels left, the shepherds went to Bethlehem to find this baby. Just as the angel said they found JESUS wrapped in cloths lying in a manger. They bowed down and worshipped Him. He was God's Son!

Before returning to the fields the shepherds shared this good news with other people. God's Son had been born!

I was so happy that God used me to tell Mary and Joseph about His plan of sending JESUS to them.

God uses angels to do many things. He wants to use everyone. How can God use you?

ASK THE CHILDREN...
"HOW CAN GOD USE YOU TO SHOW THESE QUALITIES?"

📖

Adults, now we have the opportunity to discuss with our children ways in which God can use us. We are not angels, like Gabe, but God wants us all to be His messengers. God is filled with love, joy, peace, patience, kindness, goodness, faithfulness, gentleness and self-control. (Galatians 5:22-23) These are the qualities God wants us to share with others, in order that they may see God in us.

Possible Discussion Starters:

Mommy has a headache. She is resting. What could you do to show love?

Billy, the boy next door, just came home with a new puppy. What can you do to show joy?

Daddy brought you to the park to play. Two of your friends are at the park arguing over a swing. How could you help them settle their argument showing peace?

You are playing a game with your younger brother. He seems to be taking forever to move. What can you do to show patience?

Your grandma can't find her glasses. What can you do to show kindness?

A bunch of children are throwing rocks at a house. What could you do to show goodness?

You promised Daddy to put your toys away. You are very tired. What can you do to show faithfulness?

A baby bird has fallen out of a nest. What could you do to show gentleness?

The new baby is sleeping, but you want to run through the house. How can you show self-control?

Be creative. Jot down various scenarios such as these on index cards. They are great "discussion starters." Perhaps this could be a weekly "TABLE TALK" tradition, where at some meal you have a jar with "discussion starters." Someone pulls one from the jar, it is read, then discussed during the meal.

Would love to hear from you…Together We Are Better!
e-mail us at messengergabe2015@gmail.com

Roberta Meier

Roberta Meier has worked with children and their families for over 40 years. She holds an M.A. in Education from Adelphi University in New York. Roberta founded, taught and directed Desert Springs Christian Preschool and Kindergarten in Phoenix, Arizona. Upon retirement Roberta and her husband, Ted, moved to Cornelius, North Carolina. Roberta had always wanted to write a children's book and she collaborated with a long time friend, Loretta Alexander, to write her first book, God's Special Messenger.

Loretta Alexander

Loretta Alexander is a retired art teacher and grandmother of two. She and her family moved to Arizona over 30 years ago from the Chicago area. Both Loretta's children and Roberta's children brought them together in 1979 and they have been friends ever since. Writing has been in the back of Loretta's mind for fifteen years.

Vladimir Cebu

Vladimir Cebu is an awardee graduate of the University of Saint La Salle – College of Law. Aside from being an aspiring future lawyer, he equally loves the visual arts. He owns and runs a modest advertising business in Bacolod City, Philippines, and he is very passionate about making illustrations for children's books. His works are available on Amazon and some libraries in the United States. In the future, he sees himself fighting for justice in the courts of law by day, and making illustrations for children's books by night. He can be contacted through vladimircebu@yahoo.com.

www.ingramcontent.com/pod-product-compliance
Lightning Source LLC
Chambersburg PA
CBHW040022050426
42452CB00002B/98